Healing the Hurting

Francine E. Gray

Healing the Hurting

Healing the Hurting

A Journey to Love

Francine E. Gray

Healing the Hurting

Copyright © 2016 by Francine Gray

Scriptures quotations are taken from the Holy Bible, New International Version.

Published in 2016 by *L*𝒟reams

ISBN 978-0-9851546-2-2
Library Congress catalogue number 1-3374839701

Copy Editor: Laval Belle and Sharon Debbie

Cover Design: Kingdom Scribes Publishing (KSP)

Table of Contents

Healing the Hurting

Dedication

I would like to dedicate this book to all

who have been disappointed, confused, or hurt.

May God's healing power leap through

these pages, bringing change and restoration.

Francine E. Gray

Healing the Hurting

Introduction

There were times when I felt so insignificant in this world and often wondered if anyone would miss me if I were gone. I felt very alone. There were many times I didn't feel good enough and struggled to find my way by trying to please others. *Healing The Hurting* shares many regrettable mistakes that caused me pain, shame, and guilt. My personal story is not written for shock value. I'm sharing this story with you because I am a witness you can recover from emotional pain and that God can take a dysfunctional life and make it functional. I had to learn how to forgive and let go of pride. I had to learn how to love.

Overcoming deep disappointments in people and myself was not easy. I needed healing that only God could provide. Healing was always there for the taking, I had to let go and receive God's love. Even as a "PK" (Pastor's Kid) raised in the church, I did not experience freedom. The church sometimes can only teach us so much. Our biggest growth stems from life's personal journey with God. You may fall but you get back up, multiple times. I am so grateful that He loves me in spite of all my mistakes. If I summarize my life's story in one sentence it would be, God loves me! The good news is that He loves you too!

Chapter 1
Life from the Left

My mother was told by her doctors that she couldn't have children. When she learned she was pregnant with my sister, it was a pleasant surprise, a miracle! Just as my parents were enjoying their new addition to the family, they received the news months later that she was having me. They didn't think another child would be in the future, especially so soon. The chances of having two children based on my mother's diagnosis were slim.

My parents named me after my father Frank, partly because they had hoped for a son. Family members on my father's side often called me "Frankcine". Well, another miracle happened five years later. My Dad was overjoyed to become the father of a son he thought he'd never have. We were all miracle children! The odds were against us, but we made it!

My sister and I were born 11 months apart, and as we grew up people often thought we were twins. Mom would dress us alike, but that's where our similarity ended. My sister had lighter skin and very soft, fine hair. During that time period, beauty in most communities was defined by these attributes. Having soft, fine hair and being African American meant you had *good hair*. There was a running joke in our family about my hair when I was born. The first thing the nurse told my mother was she would need to purchase a pressing comb. I had a lot of hair but it was kinky. I also had my father's darker complexion. These two factors combined did not make me feel pretty.

My sister Altha received many more compliments than I. Considered the pretty one by most, she was easily complimented by strangers. Perhaps this partly motivated me to be the smart one. My sister was also smart, but I wanted to live up to the title of smart. I learned things quickly and received praise for this trait. This positive reinforcement channeled my focus. My sister was the older pretty daughter. I was the middle child, the smart daughter, and my brother was the youngest child and the long awaited son. We all had our roles.

Altha and I were close. We shared everything, often not by choice. Sometimes I think she resented me for being born so close to her. She had a very short time span to get my parent's full attention. My brother received more special treatment than we girls because he was the boy. He had his own room with a lot more space. Overall, we loved and looked out for each other.

Part of growing up and maturing is self-discovery. It is a beautiful thing when children are allowed to grow and mature into their own person with the guidance of their parents. I was given a fraction of freedom to learn and understand who I was, but from an early age, there was also an umbrella of manipulation that shadowed my life.

13

Born Left

I was born left-handed, but I am actually right handed. Apparently, during the time of my childhood, left-handed people were considered strange or weird. Whenever I naturally used my left hand it was lightly spanked. When I held my bottle in my left hand, it was quickly removed and placed in my right hand. When I kicked out my left leg, it would be tapped so I would walk with my right one. My father did not want me to be left handed. I am sure he was trying to be helpful in his own way, but he impeded nature from taking its course. This was the beginning of constant correction. I became self-conscious and felt that I wasn't good enough.

Our family was comfortable growing up in the small suburban town of Rialto. Our neighborhood had a mixture of races. We knew our neighbors and rode our bikes in the neighborhood freely without fear. We weren't spoiled children but we didn't in truth lack for anything as far as I can recall. We got most of the Christmas gifts we asked for each year and traveled on annual family vacations to visit our aunts and uncles in the South.

While visiting I remember being treated special because we were Californians. With glowing eyes, some of my cousins would always ask "what's it like living in California?" I didn't think living in the Golden State was a big deal at the time since being raised there was all I knew. My parents made it very clear not to talk too much about what we had.

My mother stayed at home to take care of us most of the time. She eventually began working nights as a nurse and spent much of her time doing administrative work for the church. We also visited some of our sick members and would clean their houses or bring a dish. We had bake sales on some Saturdays, passed out tracts and raised funds for the church.

At the same time, my father worked for GTE, a prominent phone company at the time and worked his way up to management while also serving as a church pastor. Prior to that, he served in the Air

Force, along with my uncle. They were best friends. My father met my mother through my uncle and often joked that my mother cooked so well he had to marry her. I am not sure how true that was but my mom was great in the kitchen.

Our family had a lot of respect in our neighborhood. I would often see some of the kids in school at our church. Smart kids like me were often bullied, but I wasn't. I believe it was because I was a pastor's kid. They just didn't want to go there with me. I remember when a kid wanted to pick on me, and the biggest bully said to the kid, "No not her." It gave me a sense of security to know that someone was looking out for me. Yet, I tried to keep to myself most of the time.

I did very well in school. My first grade teacher gave me an opportunity to move up one grade level since I tested so well. My parents decided not to allow it because that would place me at the same level as my sister. They thought it would also impact my ability to fit in with other children. I didn't fit in very well with the majority of my classmates. I was quiet and shy, yet would raise my hand in class to answer questions, and sit near the front. Yes, I was the teacher's pet that would help grade papers, clean the room and sometimes would rather stay with the teacher than go to recess. I read constantly averaging a fiction novel a day.

Athleticism was not my strong point. Team captains typically picked me second to last. I took solace that at least I wasn't the last to be picked. I remember this awful attempt to win friends while in 2nd grade. The boy sitting beside me in class, always smelled of urine. Then one day, it happened. I saw the yellow puddle underneath his chair. For some reason I thought it was a good idea to tease him out loud so the other kids could hear. I yelled out "pee pee boy" as the kids laughed. He was so mad at me that he threatened to beat me up at recess. I accepted the challenge and told him I would be glad to meet him.

I'd never been in a fight before. The kids took sides and many were egging me on. I felt this rush as we walked towards the designated area where adults couldn't see. I had no fear whatsoever! I was going to win! He was taller and stronger than I, but something inside me knew I was going to unleash on him. Perhaps it was pent up anger and emotion, I am not sure. Perhaps, I just wanted a chance to be different.

So...the fight began, I was like a wild cat. I was all over him and he didn't know what hit him. The crowd eventually pulled me off him. He had scratches and was bleeding. We were both suspended. When we returned to school, I received accolades and respect from the other children. They said they didn't know I could fight like that. To be honest, I didn't either. The boy, however, was teased even more for being beat up by a girl, but not just any girl, Francine.

I started to notice that he kept to himself even more. Then he was gone...transferred to a different school. That was my first and last fight. I regretted losing control and causing such pain to another so I went back to being reserved and kept to myself. I prayed to Jesus and repented to Him on how I treated that boy. Jesus was very real to me even then. He was the only one who understood and accepted me. I couldn't really confide with others like I did with Jesus.

My father and I would often chat but there were limitations. My father really didn't like 'stupid" or 'ignorant" comments. If I made such comments, he would tell me just how stupid they were and often quoted the saying, "No one will know you are stupid until you open your mouth". He only quoted this saying if someone uttered something he considered stupid.

I was also very inquisitive and liked to question things that did not make sense to me, but had to be careful not to ask the wrong questions. I became paranoid and constantly filtered my thoughts before I spoke. If I said anything, it had to be worth saying or I would just be quiet. My feelings did not seem important. I began giving my power away by seeking the approval of others to validate my way of thinking. I began exhibiting passive aggressive traits and developed a habit of not expressing my true feelings

19

unless cornered. I began to bury my feelings and thoughts.

Why am I here?

There was a moment in my life when I considered suicide. I believe I was about ten or eleven years old and wondered if anyone would really miss me. Feeling so alone, I sat in a chair in the living room while no one else was home and imagined slitting my wrists. Sitting in a big chair with tears in my eyes, I didn't see the point of existing any longer.

I kept thinking would anyone really miss me? The room was very dark and still. Then I felt a peaceful presence. I don't recall any words being spoken, just a tremendous presence of love and comfort. I knew it was the Lord. He was more real to me at that moment, than any other time in my life. That was the first and only time I considered taking my life. I knew it was going to be okay, that He loved me unconditionally and my loneliness passed. Jesus loved and accepted me as I was.

This was very important to me at the time because I didn't think anyone loved me. Yes, they cared but there seemed to be requirements and rules. Pleasing others or constantly changing to meet their expectations was my constant. I was a people pleaser. I never said no, it was always yes.

As I matured in Christ, I realized that I mattered. My thoughts and feelings mattered. I learned that saying no is often needed to set boundaries with others. Expressing who I am, my thoughts and my feelings, is part of the freedom found in being who God created me to be.

I said the answer is No!

I had a very traditional upbringing. For example, in my early childhood we couldn't play with cards or dice because it resembled gambling. Though dancing was something I truly loved, joining dance teams, because of the "worldly" or "carnal" music was forbidden and dancing in public was a big no.

At times, I reminisce about turning the radio on in the living room to classical music, which my parents allowed. I moved the furniture around to have enough space to just dance! I don't know how flattering a dancer I was but I enjoyed it.

I joined the drill team at school without my parent's permission. We met during recess so my parents didn't notice. I was getting pretty good at it. The kids were starting to see a different side of me, and began to accept me for different reasons. It didn't last long because my sister found out and told my parents. They made me quit. I was so very disappointed. I was just getting to know girls outside of church and began showing some talent in athleticism.

I also couldn't wear fingernail polish and used crayons to color my nails. In hindsight, it must have been a strange and sorry sight but you couldn't tell me then. No it wasn't the healthiest thing to do, but I liked my red crayon nails. My mother probably saw the strange hue beginning to grow on them so I had to confess.

Most of my childhood seemed a brick wall of no, I made the best of it. The wall provided protection in a sense, it was stifling but I had my music. I didn't listen to secular music until I was a teenager and even then I listened in secret. My parents finally became a little more liberal and bought me my first radio. I was so excited; you would have thought I had a million dollars. R&B, gospel, country, and Pop tunes were my favorites. I was in my own world when I listened to music, it was so freeing.

Church Family

My church was my extended family. We were very close knit and had dinners together, laughed and cried together. We even had a green and white church van with our church name, Straight Gate C.O.G.I.C. written boldly in green. Sometimes, I didn't like the attention we got riding in the church van. My sister and I would duck at stop lights if we saw someone we knew.

The church was medium sized with white exterior, red carpet and pews. The choir wore red choir robes. I was constantly at church with all of the services we had. We had Sunday School, regular service, and night service on Sunday. We had mid-week bible study called Bible Band. We also had choir rehearsal during the same week.

When you are in a smaller church, you also learn many aspects of ministry. I was secretary, choir director, soloist, Sunday School teacher for the younger children, and maid for the church at an early age. Church was a part of my life just as much as going to school.

My Daddy, My Preacher

In spite of the many restrictions, our home was a home of love. I loved my family and my church. My father was my Pastor and a good one. He was a prolific speaker. I remember one of his sermons entitled "Put up Your Toys and Take out Your Tools." He was very funny and a down to earth teacher. I loved to hear him speak. He was my hero in more ways than one. I watched him prepare so diligently for each sermon. As a child I would lie on the floor as he studied and grabbed books from his library. I had no idea what I was reading but felt closer to him because I was studying with my Dad. He clothed himself with sincerity, really loved the Lord and cared for His people. He could do no wrong in my eyes.

There was also constant pressure as pastor's kids to uphold the image at all times. My dad often reminded me that I was his daughter which gave me a sense of pride and responsibility. I wasn't just Francine Gray; I was Pastor Gray's daughter at all times. I wore the badge with pride because I thought my dad was so great and I had to live up to a very high standard. Sometimes it seemed an overwhelming standard but I didn't want to embarrass my dad in any way.

Daddy's Gone

My image of him was changed in my late teens. One day my parents brought me and my brother into their bedroom. My sister was not living with us at the time. I noticed immediately that my mother had been crying because her eyes were swollen. I never really saw my mother cry much so it was really strange to see. At that moment, the memories flooded my mind and I began to recall that their door was shut more often. This typically meant they were going to have a private discussion or "grown folks talk" as they called it.

My dad was also working a lot of hours at his job with the phone company. I just figured he worked so many hours because we needed the money for the church and was aware of times we paid for repairs, etc, from the family budget. I would overhear conversations about how we would need to delay payment on a family bill to maintain the operation of the church.

So my parents sat us on the bed and told us that my daddy was moving out. Moving out? Yes, he's moving out! "We are going to separate for a while. It doesn't mean your dad doesn't love you, but we need some time apart. You can visit him any time." When I looked down and noticed the packed suitcases, I couldn't help but wonder how long was he going to be gone? He hugged us all, picked up his suitcases, and walked out the door.

I don't remember much about cars, but I'll never forget watching him get in his brown and tan Cadillac Seville, and drive right out of our driveway. I stood there a long time looking out the window wondering if he would change his mind but the car never came back. Questions ran through my mind, like: when will I see him again? What about the church? Is he separating from the church too? How is this going to work?

He was moving in with one of our neighbors around the corner. I remember he introduced her once as his secretary. It became very apparent that he had more than a working relationship with her. Her son went to the same school as my sister and I. He was a popular DJ and really wasn't in my low key circle of friends.

My life was turned upside down, the house became sad and empty, and I would never see my mother and father together again. I wanted what they had; the way they used to look at each other. They seemed like such a good team. Why did they have to end? I was so confused and hurt. I soon found out that he had resigned from the church.

My mom took the task of making the announcement one Sunday concerning my father's resignation. He had written a letter and she read it out loud to the church. It was a very sad and awkward day. I couldn't believe my mother had the strength to carry on with the church but she did. I believe it was in that moment hate began to enter my heart towards my father. I'm not certain this was how they both desired to approach the congregation. I just saw her alone trying to explain his decisions. How could he do this to my mother, to the church? That hatred grew in my heart and it was well seasoned with bitterness. Beneath all of these emotions, was just plain hurt.

I was truly damaged and didn't realize how much until later. Our entire family needed counseling. Unfortunately, it was not a popular option during that time. I tried to ignore my father, the cause of my pain, which seemed to be my pattern in dealing with other situations in life. Ignoring a situation or a person does not mean one is healed. As a matter of fact, ignoring a situation or person can lead to much deeper emotional and spiritual issues.

Thank God, that Jesus knew my hurt and did not give up on me. I wanted my father to hurt like I did. For at least two years, I simply ignored him. I ignored his phone calls and never went to see him. I felt like I had to choose sides so I chose my mother and the church. Anger resided in my heart, no room for love, and I didn't want anything to do with him.

The magnitude of my feelings were not realized until I had a high school writing assignment. I'll never forget this particular class. Mrs. Scambray was one of

29

the most difficult English teachers I ever had. The assignment was to write a will and testament. Simple right? We were to bequeath all of our possessions in full detail. Now mind you, we were teenagers, so we were allowed to embellish the number of possessions we had.

Along with the allotment, we wrote our last words to the ones we love. I never received an A+ on any paper from Mrs. Scambray except for this one. For some reason, I chose to unload all my thoughts and emotions regarding my family and friends including my father. To my father, I gave my best wishes and left him nothing. I wrote that he was dead to me.

We had to read our papers out loud in class and since I had an A+ I was proud to read it. I remember the moment so well, I sat on a gray stool, and began to read what I wrote about my father and surprisingly tears began to flow. I didn't feel anything while I was writing the words, but they came to life when I read them out loud. I'm sure the class didn't understand why I was crying. My teacher, however, put her arms around me, and I realized at that moment that I could no longer hold onto this hurt. I was so ashamed. It was a day that I deeply regret but thankful because God allowed me to see my heart.

So God began working on me. I realized the most important thing was not my Dad's action but my response. My response would color my future, influence my decisions and develop my character. The change didn't happen overnight; I was at least cordial to him. I started to call him to check in with him. Let's just say I gave it a half try. There were things I still needed to learn about myself that I didn't understand at the time. My heart was full of pride and self-righteousness. I discovered the hard way that forgiving my father was necessary as well as my father needing to forgive me. The phone calls were awkward at first. I felt like I was talking to a stranger.

A Whole New World

I began visiting his very nice house. He married our neighbor so now I had a step mom. She was very nice and I noticed she was very different from my Mom. She wore acrylic red nails and make up and seemed a lot more liberal. This surprised me since my parents raised me so strictly. She treated us well. We would have probably been closer if I'd met her under different circumstances. I just couldn't get rid of the thought that she took my dad away. When I visited their house, there was a new family but I felt my mother deserved to be there.

Even my dad was more liberal. I noticed he was playing R&B in his car. I also heard that he would drink alcohol on occasion. He took me to my first concert for my birthday. I will never forget that day. It was the Superfest with Luther Vandross and Patti Labelle. Luther Vandross is my favorite singer. The stage was filled with light and drama.

Both Luther and Patti changed clothes throughout the whole concert, each costume more flamboyant than the last. This was one of my greatest memories of my dad after the divorce. I never would have imagined he would take me to such a concert. Perhaps, he was trying to reintroduce himself to me. He was not the same and maybe that was not such a bad thing.

My father became a pastor in the AME church and enjoyed the freedom he had with them. The pastors were salaried so his position brought some financial stability. It took a very long time for me to visit his new church. I just didn't want to see my mother missing from this newly formed world he created. It seemed like he had moved on but I was still struggling to do so.

Chapter 2
The Lovers

Something to Prove

My mother sold the house and we moved into a three-bedroom apartment. I remember having our things on the front lawn and selling them to earn enough money to move. Sometimes I wondered why my dad appeared to be living so well while we were struggling. It wasn't easy moving away from the house where I spent most of my childhood. Yet, things were different now and many of the memories just brought sadness since a family of 5 had become a family of 4. I wanted to forget my father wasn't there. We moved close to my high school so it was much easier to get to school on my own. We all had to learn to be more independent. My mother had to work full time to pay the bills and she was still trying to help pay some of the bills for the church. We didn't see her

35

as much anymore. I had very little choice but to escape to my high school. My high school years were great. I was in the academic decathlon representing my school. I took the highest classes possible in all subject matters and was in a tight knit group of students that followed the same academic track. We became great friends, were a very competitive group and constantly compared our grades to see who was the best. It was always done in fun, at least for me.

I had an internship opportunity at UC Riverside working in a lab developing cultures in a Petri dish. It was exciting because the professor in charge of the lab stated that my work would help him publish a paper. I don't know what the paper was about but I felt valued and important. High school was my haven. I didn't have to think about my broken family.

I applied for multiple colleges and was accepted by them all. My primary choice was UCLA. GTE, my dad's place of employment, awarded me a full academic scholarship. Though I was leaning toward science and excelled in math, I wasn't certain about my major. My math teacher, Mrs. Smith held my deepest respect. She was the only female math teacher I'd ever seen. Female math teachers weren't prevalent like they are today. When I struggled with geometry in Jr. High School, my male math teacher told me girls were not good at math. This was the first time I found math so challenging so I went to him for guidance to figure out why I was having so much trouble. With a voice of pity, he said it was because women couldn't think with the left side of the brain. Being politically correct wasn't popular then so people freely spoke what they thought.

So having a female math teacher in high school was exciting for me. She only taught advanced classes. I had her every year in high school and wanted to be like her. She had power and inspired me. Now mind you, I was boxed in many times by rules and expectations from other people. Freedom to me was to be who you wanted to be and to do what you wanted to do. Freedom was power! She had a reputation for recommending her students for mathematic majors.

I was sure she would recommend me because I averaged an A- /B+ consistently. Therefore, when she came to my desk to share her recommendation, she told me not to major in math. Unbelievable! Feeling rejected was an understatement. The woman I greatly admired and respected didn't approve of me. Someone I trusted disappointed me yet again. She recommended an Asian and Caucasian student with similar grades but not me. At the time, I thought she had to be right so I declared a Premed major. That is how much respect I had of her opinion over my instinct.

I went to UCLA and began taking core classes. All premed students had to take Chemistry. The professors were very direct and said this course was designed to weed out those that should not continue in premed. I really struggled in this course and it indeed weeded me out. Premed was not for me. What major would I choose now? I reflected on Mrs.

Smith's recommendation and realized I might have been a victim of racism. This sparked even more determination to prove her wrong so I changed my major to Applied Mathematics.

Often the only black female in my math classes, I felt I had something to prove. In hindsight, I may have closed myself off from mastering other worthy subjects but because of pride, I needed to prove my academic prowess. Hindsight showed me I hadn't anything to prove at all. I wasn't exposed to many subjects but could have explored and discovered new interests. This would have been a healthy route, but I was mentally and emotionally immature, and now on the defense. Power meant proving my teacher and others like her wrong. Yet true power means following the path designed especially for me and not being afraid of new possibilities and other people's opinions.

The Lovers

My First Relationship

My mother and my brother also moved to Los Angeles when I started college. My mother felt she needed a change of scenery. I was fortunate to live in the dormitory and was able to come home on the weekends to attend church, West Angeles COGIC. It is an exciting house of worship, one of the largest churches in the area and much bigger than my family church.

My uncle, Eld. Howard Eddings had actually been a minister there and the Pastor, Bishop Charles Blake knew both of my parents. Bishop Blake was aware of my parent's divorce and was very supportive in our time of need. Here we forged new relationships. At first, it was strange for me because all I knew was my Dad as pastor but, Bishop Blake was and remains an excellent leader, which made the transition a lot easier.

I went to church on the weekends and became heavily involved in outreach ministry. I became a licensed Evangelist Missionary of the Church of God in Christ at the age of 21 and began visiting convalescent homes, women shelters, and skid row on a constant basis. I love to sing so I was also involved in various choirs and praise and worship teams. I had a very busy life. I met some of the greatest gospel artists and was honored to sing behind a few. I felt spiritually high and invincible.

As far as relationships go, I had crushes but nothing at all serious. It was just too awkward for me. I didn't attend my prom in high school and was okay with that. Asking to go wasn't a thought because I didn't think my parents would allow me to attend. My life was consistently school and church. Then I met him, let's call him Malik. He was different from the other men I encountered. He was very smart and just as talented. I was attracted to him immediately.

Malik and I became fast private friends and even faster lovers. I was striving to save myself for marriage for many years. Yet, I gave myself to someone who never mentioned anything about commitment. We had fun together and enjoyed each other's company but we didn't know each other that well. I ignored so many red flags. My pride thought our situation would be different in spite of all the blaring flags.   I was free with him and could be myself.   There goes that feeling of power and freedom. I also had never known such strong passion. I thought it must be love. I learned much later that you could have passion for someone and assume it is love. Passion comes and goes, real love takes sacrifice and commitment.

I was still somewhat estranged from my father when I met Malik and missed my talks with him, but I could talk to Malik about most things.   I didn't pray much about our developing relationship. I made excuses for our fornication and began   playing with fire.   I was blinded by my emotions and naivety.

As a result, I continued seeing Malik.   When I saw him at church, I knew it was on.   I had a false sense of security thinking he loved me. I would wait for the call in the late evening and I was there. I began telling my friends I was seeing someone.   Word got back to him and he immediately corrected me saying *"no we are not seeing each other; we are dating each other. We are free to date other people"*. He was sleeping with me! Didn't that automatically mean we were seeing each other? I had a lot to learn.

The irony is that he never lied to me. I just didn't ask the right questions and made assumptions. I let my guard down with him because I was naïve and thought men in the church were safer. I had no practice dating. Having to worry about unclear signals from a man in church didn't cross my mind. I didn't talk to my mother because I didn't want her to be disappointed in me. Again, there was so much to learn. I had to learn to set boundaries, not make assumptions and not to relinquish total control to a man. The Holy Spirit had to remain in the driver's seat, even in dating. I trusted God with other areas of my life but didn't trust Him in dating.

So the day came and I got the *"it's not you but me"* speech, he said we should see other people and that I deserved to be with someone that will love me the way I deserved to be loved. This utterly broke my heart. Yet why was I surprised? Every rule in the relationship book was broken and I felt like a fool. Had I saved my virginity for so many years to give myself to the wrong man? What happened to my being so smart?

Healing was certainly a necessary priority but I didn't seek it then. Sharing what happened with a few close friends and never seeking counsel was the immediate remedy. Healing for my broken heart was a fix but it ran much deeper than that. I still needed healing for my prideful heart. I needed help.

Broken Love

I took my brokenness to another man outside of church. I needed a smog check one day and went to an auto shop. The man who greeted me was a very handsome and charming guy. Andrew said he didn't go to church much but he was spiritual. At this point, it didn't matter where I met a man since the man I met previously in church seemed to have the same standards. What I liked most about Andrew was that he was openly affectionate, no more dodging and hiding. I told my mother about him. He treated me very well. I thought I was in love again and enjoyed how he made me feel but still didn't understand what love looked like. He and I had a sexual relationship very soon in the relationship. I made excuses every time guilt rose in my heart. Since Andrew loved me, God must be okay with it. I thought he would marry me eventually so it was all right to be intimate. Andrew actually mentioned our future together and we would daydream about our tomorrow. Talking about marriage and being married of course are two different things.

I was not submitting my body faithfully to God. Romans 12:1, *Therefore, I urge you, brothers and sisters, in view of God's mercy, to offer your bodies as a living sacrifice, holy and pleasing to God--this is your true and proper worship.* If I didn't learn how to submit my body to God being single, could I truly submit my body solely to my future husband? Would I come up with excuses in my marriage to defile the marriage bed? I have learned not to assume that I am not capable of the greatest of sins. In God's eyes, a sin is a sin. I realize that I am more than capable of any sin and it is best that I do things God's way and choose His holy path for my life. I eventually learned to apply His Word to my life to live free of fornication. I had to let His light shine even in the dark corners of my heart.

Now at this point in my life, I still was not communicating with my father about my relationships with men. Maybe if I did, I would have made different choices. Yet pride prevented me from sharing with my father or even asking for advice. I was still involved in the ministry and never skipped a beat. Then the day came that I found out I was pregnant.

Who is the Daddy?

I was shocked and met my brother to drop the bomb over Shakey's pizza. He was in mid slice as he looked at me in disbelief. He gave me a bear hug and asked me what I was going to do. I will never forget that crucial day. He told me that whatever I decided he would be there for me. Those words were so reassuring to me because I felt terribly alone and full of shame and regret.

When I shared the news with Andrew he didn't believe me at first. The doctor told him that he could not have children for medical reasons. He also didn't believe because there was a slight chance the baby was not his. Malik had called me one night; I hadn't seen him in many months. I told him that I was with someone but he said he just wanted to talk. After all, I did miss our talks and it would be nice to talk just to see what he was up to, but it was a very bad idea. I should have known better.

That night I cheated. It was not my intention for anything to happen. Did I still have feelings for him? Why did I even go? I felt so guilty that I confessed our encounter that night with Andrew. I never thought I would cheat on anyone, especially Andrew and on top of it, I couldn't help but thinking I judged my father for cheating on my mother. What a hypocrite; I was no different. Andrew forgave but didn't forget, he had legitimate doubt.

I wore my shame like a cloak and remembered reading the Scarlet Letter in high school. The town had forced Hester to wear a Scarlet letter on her clothing to show everyone that she was an adulterer. Like the character Hester Prynne, my pregnant belly would be my scarlet letter because I decided to keep the child and come clean. Finally, the truth as painful as it was, would be out for all the world to see.

Love at First sight

I was a broken woman throughout my pregnancy, 25 years old and battling depression. I attended Lamaze classes by myself. Malik kept his distance but called every now and again to check up on me. Andrew did the same. Neither offered real assistance. Someone gave me a book about what to expect when expecting. I read it front to back. It helped but there was no comfort in it. Moving back home with my mother felt like complete failure. I didn't want to be a burden. My brother would help out as he could.

When the day came to finally deliver, my mother was in the delivery room. Her first words to me were "call the 'yellow one", (Andrew), he is the father". When I had a chance to look at my beautiful baby girl, Andrew and Malik were far from my mind. I knew it was me and her. I didn't know what tomorrow was going to bring but I was going to love and protect her with all that I had in me. I knew my life was never going to be the same. There were more mountains in my life but she inspired me to climb. It was love at first sight; a pure love I'd never experienced before. The eyes looking back at me didn't care about my past or my shortcomings, I was her mother. I was going to try my best to be the best mother that I could be.

Healing the Hurting

50

The Lovers

Chapter 3
Backs Turned Away

Let me back up a few months and explain my experience with the church during pregnancy. My mother was a leader in the church so telling her was so very hard. She still thought I was virgin. I knew she had the vision of a wedding with me all in white and a Pastor waiting for me at the altar. That vision became a little cracked after my announcement. I wouldn't call my mother a fragile woman but she experienced so much disappointment in her life. I didn't want to be one of them.

After the shock of my announcement wore off, she professed she would be there for me. I actually didn't know how she would react to my pregnancy because I knew she would be very worried about the church's reaction toward both of us. She had high hopes for me. I typically did what she expected of me so to

51

admit I wasn't a virgin anymore and pregnant was a double shock. I never thought she would understand even though she said she was going to be there for me. She never shared any stories of her dating struggles. I thought it was really hard for her to relate to my pregnancy.

The Scarlet Belly

I also went to my spiritual mentor. I valued her advice and guidance, and highly respected her wisdom. She was another woman I saw living in freedom. She had freedom in her ministry. I'd never met anyone quite like her. We met in her office and I told her the news with tears in my eyes. She asked me the typical questions, who is the father? Does he go to this church? How long have I been sleeping with him?

She then went into a monologue regarding open repentance. She said because of my hidden sin that I must openly demonstrate my repentance. Again, this sounded like The Scarlet Letter being lived out by me.

The stance she proposed was a little confusing. I would think that my protruding belly would be enough of a visible demonstration. Everyone knew I wasn't married. I told her I repented from my sin and was seeking spiritual guidance. I received no comfort whatsoever from her. I didn't receive the loving arms of restoration I'd expected, yet I didn't feel that I had a right to question her judgment.

Things began to change very quickly. Before the meeting with her, I was on the mailing and call lists to stay informed of the latest news. As I began to show, I began to hear of meetings I wasn't invited to. We had a roster and I noticed my name was simply not there. There was no proactive notification. Again, no gesture of acknowledgement of possible restoration. I felt totally abandoned by the person I respected so much. I stopped doing outreach ministry as well. What would a failure have to say to anyone?

I endured the stares, whispers and avoidance as my belly began to grow. There were looks of pity and even saw a few looks of satisfaction. It was if they were saying, "I knew it!". The experience was miserable. Yet, as the baby began to kick, my focus changed to the wonderful life inside of me. It seemed she was telling me, "Wake up, I am here." It wasn't the baby's fault the situation was almost unbearable. I determined my child was not going to ever feel less than because of my mistakes.

The Loving Few

I must admit that there were jewels in my life. Those that really helped me. One of many examples was a testimony from Mother Minerva Franklin. I was sitting on the front pew after a service waiting for my mother. I was far along and didn't drive much then. She hugged me, sat down and said *"You know Francine; you will survive this. I've been where you are"*. I was shocked because I really didn't know her story. She was the last person I thought would have been in my situation. She shared how she had a child before marriage and understood the difficulty. She told me that "God forgives and you have to forgive yourself".

54

Mother Franklin has passed and is now in God's heavenly arms. I will never forget her simple share that turned my life around. Who knew that a testimony like hers would be so liberating. I wasn't alone. Someone actually admitted they made the same mistake and survived. She gave me hope.

There was also Stephanie Shelling. I actually had no plans for a baby shower. Who in the world would throw me a shower? To my surprise she did. I found out later there were some who refused to come to my shower because they felt it would condone having children out of wedlock. Yet, in spite of the negativity, I had a really nice baby shower and it helped me focus on the life inside me and the few friends that actually loved and cared for me and the baby.

Church People Hurt

The church hurt was real. Perhaps, it hurt so much because it was so unexpected. I knew those around me would be disappointed but not uncaring. I let my guard down and had high expectations of those around me. They didn't understand that I was already hard on myself. I just needed love. So how did I overcome the church hurt? It wasn't easy and it wasn't quick. The Holy Spirit revealed to me that those who inflict pain are hurting themselves.

So the women who didn't attend the shower because of their so called convictions, were insensitive and probably had their own issues around unwed pregnancies. As Jesus instructs on the cross, I have to forgive because they did not understand the impact of their heartless decisions. The mentor who treated me so coldly probably had her own love issues. When you truly understand and receive the love of God, it will reflect in how you treat others. This is a basic biblical truth. As a matter of fact, before I was broken I had the same unfruitful religious response to others as well. She actually reminded me of myself before I realized my own capacity for sin and totally received the love of Christ.

The scripture says that the church consists of the wheat and the tare. At that time, she was a tare in my life. Mother Franklin was the wheat. She was a builder of God's kingdom and I was forever edified by just one encounter with her. The experience taught me to become a builder and not a destroyer. I know what it feels like to be torn down. Part of my healing process is to help others who feel torn down. When I help others, it makes me stronger. I know I am not alone and I want you to know that you are not alone either.

God is perfect love. People may disappoint you but they are not God. God loves us in spite of our imperfections. We have to love others in spite of their imperfections. When we accept His love, we begin to love ourselves and others around us.

Healing the Hurting

Backs Turned Away

Chapter 4
Tried to Find My Way in the Dark

I took Eliza home from the hospital and was ready to start my new life as a mom, yet was on the defensive; I didn't expect anything from anyone and was so protective of my daughter that I did not want her to feel less valued because I was a single mother. I was constantly fighting this emotion within myself. This defensive emotion influenced some of my decisions in raising Eliza.

Before my pregnancy, I worked in the retirement plan field. I was hired right after college and was planning to be an actuary. An actuary utilizes mathematical tools to measure risk in the financial arena. However, after Eliza's birth, I totally changed my career path from the retirement field to teaching. I had no idea how to be a mother and hoped I could gain experience with other children who were older. I took the necessary exams and earned my temporary teaching credential.

I was on welfare during that time and wasn't getting much child support to take care of her. Being on welfare, was very humbling for me. I waited in line for food stamps with shame. I never thought I would need it but was willing to do what I had to do to care for my daughter.

The Teacher

My first job as a teacher was at Berendo Middle School in Los Angeles, CA. I realized how much I really enjoyed teaching and preparing for each lesson. Teaching outside of the box was a joy. I wanted everyone in my class to know they could do math because I remembered the negativity I experienced as a young girl. I created projects they could relate to in their world.

It was fun to see their smiles after learning the concepts. I loved bonding with the children. It felt good to be needed. I was starting to feel successful again. Those children definitely valued my sincere teaching approach. Often times, they would stay after school or stay during their lunch period just to hang around or to ask questions about their homework assignments. It gave me confidence.

Time to Move

The tremendous cost of raising a child was monumental. I worked overtime to pay expenses and spent more time at work with other children than my own. The pay wasn't that great so a change was necessary. I stopped attending church as much, and decided to go back into the financial industry using a job placement agency that found me a position in Yakima, Washington. The job offered more salary and I decided to take it. My brother helped by babysitting Eliza. I told him about the opportunity and he said he'd come with us. I would have never asked him to come but so glad he did.

He did so much already. He was only 21 and I really didn't want to be a burden. To be honest, Frank demonstrated a commitment to me and my daughter that I never experienced before. I will forever be indebted to him. He lived with us during most of Eliza's early childhood. We both worked and took care of her in shifts. My daughter still considers him like a father. I felt jaded when it came to trusting men but my brother was such a great example of a loving Godly male.

We lived in Yakima, Washington for a year. The job was great but I was lonely. My brother was lonely too. There weren't many African Americans in Yakima but we tried to make it work. We joined a small church and the people were very nice, but something was still missing. The money was sufficient to take care of Eliza but being there didn't feel right. The idea hit me to move to Texas. I was a great admirer of Bishop Jakes and heard his church was there. I'd also read that the job market was great. I still had my savings and found an apartment online. So we packed our bags and moved. Mind you, I didn't have a job yet. It was risky but I wanted to go.

When we arrived, I looked in the phone book for local firms that administered 401k plans, called Cecil & Company and spoke with the manager. I told her about my job experience, she arranged a meeting with me and offered me a job on the spot. I knew the Lord was with me. I don't recommend moving without a job to anyone, but it worked out for us. I worked there for a year then left to take a job at Fidelity Investments.

Fidelity is where I met one of my best friends, Cordelia West. She was a coworker of mine and we became fast friends. She called everyone Sunshine. She was like sunshine in my life. Cordelia often gave sound wisdom about the little things in life that were helpful for a new mom. She raised children of her own so I began to rely on her advice often. Some things you can't learn from a book and it seemed I had a book for everything. She was very easy to talk to and a girlfriend in the time of need. She accepted and loved me for who I was with all my flaws.

Fidelity was also where I met Lori McCarthy. She wanted to sell her house and asked if I was interested in buying it. I wasn't thinking about owning my own home but thought, why not. I knew it was better to be a home owner. We went through the process and I purchased my first home! This was a huge milestone for me. I was a single mother with my first home! It took a lot of work to keep the house going but my brother helped out a lot. It was beautiful two story house in a great neighborhood. The school district was great and I finally felt that I was in a stable place where my daughter could grow up.

The Handy Man

I still wasn't ready to date yet, but I did anyway. I still had anger and bitterness in my heart. I also didn't have a healthy image of myself. I didn't think I deserved the quality of man I use to dream about. I was lonely so I thought I'd try meeting someone online. I met a man named Wallace and exchanged information with him. After two days talking over the phone, we decided to meet at Starbucks.

He was a year younger than I, handsome with a beautiful smile and so easy to talk to. Wallace was different than the type of guys I normally dated but he was interesting. We dated for about six months and decided to try a monogamous relationship. Wallace had various jobs in warehouses as a fork lift operator. He did not have a formal education but was handy with his hands and liked fixing things. He didn't attend church much and neither did I at that time. Wallace made me laugh, he took me fishing and we genuinely had fun together. I thought I had found my happy ending. But yet again, I ignored red flags.

My daughter did not like him much. He was an alcoholic. Wallace drank beer day and night and every time I saw him he had a drink in his hand. I decided to take my first drink with him. I never desired to drink but there was so much alcohol around, it just seemed the natural thing to do. I didn't like the taste of alcohol much so it was short lived.

We became closer but he couldn't keep a job which made it nearly impossible to plan a future together. By this time, my brother moved to Kansas for a job opportunity. When he left, my boyfriend moved in. I missed having a man around and thought it would be a good idea for Wallace to move in and help around the house since he was so good with his hands.

Wallace was living with his sister when I met him. He babysat his nephew often so his nephew was constantly around Eliza and I. I didn't mind because he was a very adorable kid. I think he was about 3 or 4 years old. We took several road trips together. It felt like we were building a family. Many times we traveled to see his mother in Arkansas. His mother and I hit it off well. She liked me so much that one time she pulled me aside and asked why I was with Wallace. She said someone is going to kill him one day. I really didn't understand what she was trying to say at the time.

One day Wallace picked me up from work. We were sitting in the car and he turned to me and said, "I have a gift for you". I was still putting on my seat belt. I looked, and to my surprise saw an engagement ring. It was small and beautiful. He said, "I wanted to get you something better but would you marry me?" I immediately said yes even though we still had our problems.

I will never forget the one and only session of premarital counseling. It was a disaster! The marriage counselor was an ex-coworker of mine. He worked in the HR department. I didn't know him well but remembered him and had no idea he was the counselor until we arrived. He was surprised to see me. I wasn't aware he had chosen counseling as his new career. There was a point in the session when he asked us to take a piece of paper and write the definition of intimacy in our own words.

I was on one side of the room writing vigorously on how closeness is a determining factor of intimacy and blah blah blah. I noticed my fiancé was staring at me after a couple of minutes. I asked are you done? He said yes, and why wasn't I done? I went ahead and finished my masterpiece dissertation on intimacy. The counselor told us to exchange our notes. The only thing that he had on his piece of paper was SEX. I just looked at him in disbelief. He was honest. It is what he thought. I realized the closeness I thought we had was centered around sex yet again. I was still making the same mistakes. He was just honest about it. We stayed together for a couple of weeks after this but we both knew we weren't the same.

The end came when I got a call from a woman who was looking for Wallace. She called me wondering who I was. She found my number in her boyfriend's phone. I asked her, "your boyfriend is who exactly?" She said Wallace. After our comparison of notes, I packed his clothes and dumped them on his sister's front yard in the middle of the night.

Pregnant Again?

I must admit, this time, I was at my lowest, emotionally and spiritually. I felt rejected once again and became very self-absorbed. It was about me at this point. Finding out I was pregnant was the worst news that I could get. I barely had enough emotional stamina to raise my daughter and the expenses were high. I also wasn't getting consistent child support. The soon to be father couldn't hold a stable job and he betrayed me. I did not want anything to do with him. I couldn't imagine having two children. So, I did the unthinkable, I Made The Call. I was seven weeks pregnant. I was in a fog with no desire to pray because I already knew the answer. I didn't want to exercise faith. I just wanted to be free.

I set myself free (with the help of doctors) but immediately was bound by even more guilt and shame. I deserved to be bound by guilt and shame. I murdered my own child. My own flesh and blood, a gift from God in spite of my sinful actions. God is the giver of life and I took a life. It didn't take long for depression to sweep in. I attended the Potter's House every now and then but didn't feel the same. I never felt unworthy to go to church before but I did this time.

Stress is a silent killer; to me abortion is also a silent killer that I allowed to happen in secret and darkness. I even heard someone say that mothers who have committed abortion should be jailed or killed. This part of my life is the hardest to share. Did I feel like a monster? Yes, I did. Do I regret my decision? Yes, even to this day.

Showers of Love Against Shame

What made matters worse is that I never told the father and never considered his feelings. Eventually, I knew I had to tell him. He was driving when I told him I had something very serious to share with him. After sharing the sordid details, the phone became deadly quiet. I called his name. In the softest voice I ever heard from him, he said, "I am crying Francine". He'd never had children and said he would have taken care of the child even if I didn't want to. Knowing Wallace, he probably would have. Most likely, the child would have had a rough life but would have had a life. The magnitude of my decision hit me like a ton of bricks.

The moment I hung up the phone with Wallace, I finally prayed, broken and full of guilt and shame. I never thought in a million years I would take a life but I did. In spite of it all, when I prayed, God's love and peace washed over me like a shower. This was a pivotal moment in my walk with Christ because I really understood salvation. A much needed salvation. A much needed healing.

I was guilty, plain and simple. God forgave me! He still loved me! I never felt so grateful for such an undeserved pardon. My religious pride was broken. I fully understood I was a sinner saved by grace. I realized God knew exactly the decisions I would make even though I didn't. He loved me in spite of all my hypocrisy, pride, fear, and doubt. This scripture found in Luke 15.7, where Jesus talked about the lost sheep came to mind. *"I tell you that in the same way there will be more rejoicing in heaven over one sinner who repents than over ninety-nine righteous persons who do not need to repent."* In spite of all my mistakes, His plans for me haven't changed; neither have his plans for you.

Chapter 5

Let the Healing Begin

Enosh

I decided to name our lost child Enosh. Enosh means mankind. I wasn't far along enough to determine the gender of our child, but our baby deserved a name. It's difficult to honor the memory of Enosh after the abortion, a regrettable term for such a regrettable action. However, I honor Enosh by sharing this life with you. After writing and sharing this story with you, I feel led to help other expecting mothers who encounter the same experiences. If you are encountering the same challenge in your life, I highly recommend you find some way to honor your child. God may show you a different way but I am confident that He will show you a way.

Earlier this year, God gave me a vision of stars in the sky. I didn't understand what the vision meant at first. I relayed the entire vision to a minister friend of mine who interprets dreams and visions. His interpretation was, my ministry would reach outside the four walls of the church. In the vision, I was ministering in a church without a ceiling. All I could see was a plethora of stars but there was this one shining star that came down. When it came down, the doors of the church were opened and the church was filled with light. I saw people rushing inside the church.

The minister said the stars represent the lives of those whom would be touched by my story. Those lives include the children who now have a chance to live because I decided to share my story. This inspires me. I know my story will benefit others to help make better choices. I could keep this part of my past secret like so many other women do even today in the church. But my sharing my story, is part of my healing. If you have had a similar experience, be

74

assured that healing is available for you. Burying the memory is not healing, sharing the truth is.

I was determined not to live in condemnation. God does not condemn but He convicts. God showed me there was a brighter future. I proceeded to go back to church and decided not to date until I was ready. It took some time, but I was able to find a life rhythm. I did inform my parents of the abortion. My mother and father were saddened I did not come to them earlier but were both very supportive during that time.

His Image

I mentioned how much I wanted power earlier. Now I understand that I always had power. I always had the power to be who God created me to be. This power was always available but I didn't exercise my faith. I understand my self-worth. These two scriptures come to mind:

Jeremiah 1:5 – Before I formed you in the womb I knew you, and before you were born I consecrated you; I

Let the Healing Begin

appointed you a prophet to the nations. Matthew 10:29-31 – Are not two sparrows sold for a penny? And not one of them will fall to the ground apart from your Father. But even the hairs of your head are all numbered. Fear not, therefore; you are of more value than many sparrows.

Family and friends, no matter how much they love us, don't determine our true value. I ran into trouble when I allowed the assessments of others to determine my life. My own assessment was not good enough either. The key to my healing and emotional freedom is to see myself as God sees me.

Coming Home

I called up an old friend in California because I was curious to see how he was doing. He was a minister and was doing some amazing things in the community. He asked me how I was doing and I shared with him about the challenges I endured while living in Texas. He was surprised but non-judgmental. I left California without saying good bye to him and others. That was something I truly regret.

After talking with him, I knew I had to come back home. I wasn't on the defense anymore. I didn't have to run away. I didn't have anything to prove. I just wanted to help others in any way I could.

My brother came from Kansas to help pack and move Eliza and myself back to California. I sold my house in Fort Worth and got a job with Transamerica in Los Angeles. Leaving all the friends I developed in Texas was tough, yet I knew it was time to go. A large part of my healing was to return home. Being back home after 8 years felt strange. Some of my friends had moved away so new relationships had to be established once more. I was a different person now, I knew God's grace first hand and wasn't going to allow religion to guide me, but God's love and kindness.

Healing the Hurting

Let the Healing Begin

Chapter 6

Helping the Hurting

I can truly say my ministry was conceived after my darkest hour. Now, I seek those who are hurting to share the spiritual medicine ready for the taking. I returned to ministry with humility and a better understanding. Now when I see hurting people, I see myself.

One dear sister comes to mind, Tasha. One Sunday morning on my way to class, I saw a very disoriented Tasha coming out of the sanctuary. She was mumbling rapidly, "hospital, respiratory problems, just left the hospital, need to go to take insulin soon…don't want to go home but had to come to church …I don't want to die today". I was thinking to myself, I need to slow her down because she was

79

breathing so heavily. She was in tears and needed help.

My first concern was her health and I asked her how could I assist. She said she didn't know, she left her insulin at home but wanted to come to church. I prayed for her and she finally calmed down. I invited her to my Sunday school class and she agreed to come. This was a women's bible class but open to everyone. It was the first Sunday of the month and traditionally the women wore all white. The subject of the day was Faith and Healing. My mother happened to be teaching that day. Tasha was listening as I held her hand. She whispered in my ear and asked, "Can we go outside?"

Still holding her hand, I led her outside so we could talk. She didn't feel comfortable with the way she was dressed. She mentioned she was not like me or them. She leaned on me and told me her story. She said she was an abomination! I never heard anyone use that term to describe themselves before, my heart was pierced. I asked her why she felt that way.

Tasha was raped by her father and two brothers multiple times when she was a teenager. This activity went on for many years, and she eventually became pregnant. Tasha told her mother but she didn't believe her. Her mother was a religious woman, accused Tasha of lying and forced her to keep the child knowing the father was a family member.

She hated her family and felt estranged from her daughter. As she finished sharing her story, I looked through the window and noticed the class was standing up for prayer. I wanted her to be a part of the prayer so we went back inside. A circle of women including myself began to pray. A spiritual battle ensued that took some time but she eventually gave her life to Christ and forgave her mother. Jesus can help through the forgiving process starting with the heart first.

Helping the Hurting

As explained earlier, I was not a forgiving person because I did not look in the mirror to see that I needed forgiveness too. I am not perfect by any means. Every person, no matter how good they think they are needs forgiveness, most importantly God's forgiveness. A large part of our healing calls for a commitment of forgiveness.

"Get rid of all bitterness, rage and anger, brawling and slander, along with every form of malice. Be kind and compassionate to one another, forgiving each other, just as in Christ God forgave you." Ephesians 4:31-32

I gave Tasha a ride home because I wanted to make sure she took her insulin and to bless her home. On the way, I asked about her daughter and if her daughter knew the circumstances surrounding her birth.

Tasha said yes, her mother told her daughter when she was seven years old. My heart was pierced again knowing her daughter was living with the stigma of being a product of incest. If the mother felt like an abomination, I wondered how the daughter felt? We pulled up and saw a women dressed in all black walking on the sidewalk. Tasha said, "I think I know her. I think that is my daughter". She hadn't seen or heard from her daughter in months and there she was walking towards her house. She was shocked and so was I.

I was glad I had a golden opportunity to meet this young lady. We went upstairs after introductions. I immediately discerned the sweet heart of the woman who was dirty and smelled. She looked like she was living on the streets. We prayed in a circle for the house and each other. My daughter was with me and she began to testify and preach. Tasha's daughter was listening attentively. Eliza hugged her and we began to talk about mothers and daughters. It appeared they didn't have a God centered relationship.

This mother and daughter, did not know their self-worth. Their lives reflected this through various addictions and lifestyle choices. Both women were abused and began abusing themselves and each other. Now God can show them a better path, a path of love and peace. Now they can see themselves as God sees them and accept His unconditional love.

My True Love

I found my true love. Finding true love was not easy for me. We all have misconceptions about love. I certainly didn't experience love in dysfunctional relationships. I thought if I pleased a man and gave him everything he wanted, I would get love in return. I didn't have to compromise or dishonor my body for the company of a man. I was taught at an early age, that my body is the temple of the Lord. When I dishonored my body, I dishonored God. I knew better but didn't exercise my convictions. Drinking and going to places like a club was not and is not who I am. If someone cannot enjoy my company for who I am, then that person is not worthy of my company at all. Call me a church girl, a bible reader, a preacher's kid, a prayer warrior, a Child of God, yes, I am all of the above. I love God and God loves me and those dysfunctional experiences have taught me to love Him even more. I am who God says I am, I have what God says I have, I can do what God says I can do, now I am going where God tells me to go.

The spirit of a man will sustain him in sickness, But who can bear a broken spirt? Proverbs 18:14

As you can see, my brokenness began at an early age. My father telling me I was right-handed when I am left-handed, the divorce, the loss of our church, discouragement of teachers, certain church people, and so called friends all played a role in my hurt, not to mention the broken engagement and loss of my child. But, God was always there even through the darkest moments, God was healing my hurt.

I know He is with me all the way. I can always go to Him and don't have to hide but can come boldly to the throne of grace. The love of family and friends has its limits, but God's love is limitless. His grace covered my shame and hurt. He empowers me to love. Through my journey I learned about love and how to show love. I made a commitment to love God and myself. I learned how to trust His love and have faith. When I submitted to His wisdom and guidance, I found happiness, joy, peace, and rest. He was giving me a model of love by His enduring loving for me.

I Corinthians 13:4-8 Love suffers long and is kind; love does not envy; love does not parade itself; is not puffed up; does not behave rudely, does not seek his own, is not provoked, thinks no evil; does not rejoice in iniquity, but rejoices in the truth; bears all things, believes all things, hope all things, endures all things. Love never fails.

Chapter 7

So Now What?

Sharing my story with you, is the most difficult thing I've ever done in my life. It's difficult because I've never shared so many intimate details before. Some of those life experiences were quite painful. I was not sure how you would receive my story. Yet, I'm so glad I did. *And they overcame him by the blood of the Lamb and the word of their testimony, Revelation 12:11.* My transparent testimony empowered my life. Now, I really understand the necessity of testimonies in the body of Christ.

Remembering Daddy

My father passed away July 6, 2009. I wish I'd spent more time with him. Once I got pass the bitterness, I enjoyed his wisdom and guidance. Our relationship matured and I began to know him as an adult. We weren't just father and daughter anymore but friends too. Daddy started spending time with Eliza and built a relationship with her as well. I still remember his beautiful funeral. He was pastoring an AME church at that time. I heard so many testimonies on how he touched so many lives. The representatives of the Air Force also reminded us of his service to our country.

Through my healing, I realized that my father wasn't a perfect man, only Jesus is. I know that he loved God, he loved his family, he loved his country, he loved God's people and he loved me. I am so very proud to call my father a good man. I miss him so very much and grateful I had an opportunity to restore and rebuild our relationship. I think about him constantly and encourage you to cherish the time with your loved ones as well. Tomorrow is not promised to any of us.

So Now What?

Eliza

I am very proud of my daughter, Eliza. She has grown into a very beautiful and well-balanced young lady. I strived to be attentive to her interests and encouraged her to explore all of them. There is no such thing as a perfect parent, I just want the best for her. I did not want her to have the baggage I carried for so many years. She has become quite a prolific artist. I remember her carrying a pad and pencil everywhere she went. I didn't have to pack toys just materials to sketch.

I continue to encourage her to explore her gifts and take risks. My desire is that she be herself. I witnessed her develop her own relationship with God. I can't be more excited about that. Her father and his family are also developing a better relationship with her. I am very grateful that God took such a rocky beginning and gave her what she needed.

Relationships

While writing this book, I prayed about how I should view my past relationships. I believe I loved each one but from a broken place. I heard someone say once that hurt people will hurt people. My whole outlook has changed. *Proverbs 12:26 says the righteous choose their friends carefully.* I am constantly presented with choices of who I should befriend. I have learned to choose carefully. I pray about my friendships both male and female. I understand now that His plan for my life is my guiding light. I now build Godly relationships in my life. I seek God to understand the roles that individuals play in my life. Some may be acquaintances, mentors, or friends. Today, I allow God to help me determine the differences. I am in a much healthier place than before. The Lord has brought me a long way. I believe that one day I will have my lifetime friend, my husband. I know I am on the right track. In the meantime, I am enjoying the journey focusing on my gifts and my purpose. *But*

So Now What?

seek first his kingdom and his righteousness, and all these things will be given to you as well. Matthew 6:33(NIV)

Sharing the gift

I came back to my home church, West Angeles COGIC, a much-changed woman and ready to serve. Driven to obey God and follow His path for my life, heavily involved in teaching His word, working in outreach ministry and sharing the gospel and my story. Until I take my last breath if I can help someone who is hurting, I will. I no longer seek the validation of people anymore. I realize there will always be those who don't understand you, will talk about you, and may even try to block you. It doesn't matter. My confidence, power and approval comes from God. John 8:36, So if the Son sets you free, you will be free indeed.

I have embraced the gifts he instilled in me. The spiritual gift of healing in particular is special to me. It is not a coincidence that I had to be broken so that this gift could flourish through me. I had to

91

experience healing first hand. I remember as a small child, God would tell me to lay hands on particular people.

There were times when my hands were literally hot and red but I didn't obey because of fear and not wanting people to think I was crazy. I was looking within and worried about people. Now I willingly operate in the gift he has given me. The healing gift is the impetus for this book. He showed me that many would be healed through my story. I am excited about my future and where He is taking me and have a story of victory.

My story may not have mirrored that of a great person, but it is my hope that God appears great in these pages. I am nothing without Christ. John 15:5 "I am the vine; you are the branches. If you remain in me and I in you, you will bear much fruit; apart from me you can do nothing". I pray that you've been edified and healed through my sharing. It is a story of hope, forgiveness, love and healing. I know I'll never be the same.

So Now What?

About the Author

Francine E. Gray, MAEd is a public speaker and teacher, well known for her ability to relay topics with clarity, inspiring those around her. She has taught classes that vary from spiritual growth and empowerment to financial freedom, is a manager with over 20 years of financial experience and a certified financial instructor. Her volunteer efforts in financial literacy were featured in a national blog by Transamerica Solutions in 2015 which won her Educator of the Year award.

For more information on speaking and seminars, contact helpbuildothers@gmail.com